NEW ZEALAND
SHRUBS
& SMALL TREES

MURDOCH RILEY

In appreciation of the beauty of
New Zealand's shrubs, small trees
and other unique plants.

Illustrations by P. F. Scaife

FLOWERING CLIMBERS — PAGES 4-13
SHRUBS AND SMALL TREES — PAGES 14-51
WILD ORCHIDS — PAGES 52 on

VIKING SEVENSEAS LTD;
WELLINGTON, NEW ZEALAND.

COMMON AND SCIENTIFIC NAME INDEX

Aporostylis bifolia	52
Avicennia resinfera	47
Bearded Greenhood Orchid	55
Blue Sun Orchid	54
Brachyglottis kirkii	43
Brachyglottis rotundifolia	42
Buddleia Corokia	29
Bulb Leaf Orchid	57, Back Cover
Bulbophyllum pygmaeum	57, Back Cover
Bullibul	46
Bundle Flowered Mingimingi	32
Bush Lawyer	10
Cabbage Tree	48, 49
Chiloglottis cornuta	52
Clematis	5
Clematis forsteri	5
Clematis paniculata	4, 5
Clianthus puniceus	19
Coastal Koromiko	44, 45
Common Greenhood Orchid	55
Common Leek Orchid	56
Common Onion Orchid	56
Coprosma acerosa	38, 39
Coprosma foetissima	38, 39
Coprosma grandifolia	37
Coprosma lucida	39
Cordyline australis	48, 49
Cordyline indivisa	49
Cordyline pumilio	48, 49
Cork Tree	18
Corokia buddleioides	29
Corokia cotonester	28
Corybas micranthus	53
Corybas oblongus	53
Corybas rivularis	53
Corybas tribolus	53
Cotton Wood	22
Cyathodes junipera	33
Daisy Shrub	43
Dancing Spider Orchid	53
Dendrobium cunninghamii	52
Discaria toumatou	21
Dracophyllum latifolium	34, 35
Dracophyllum longifolium	34
Dracophyllum traversii	34, 35
Dwarf Cabbage Tree	48, 49
Earina autumnalis	57, Back Cover
Earina mucronata	57, Back Cover
Easter Orchid	57, Back Cover
Entelea arborescens	18
Five Finger	27
Flax	50
Freycinetia baueriana, (ssp. banksii)	13
Gastrodia cunninghamii	57
Gastrodia minor	57
Gaultheria antipoda	30, 31
Gaultheria depressa, (var. novae-zelandiae)	31
Geniostoma rupestre	13
Golden Corokia	28
Grass Tree	34
Green Bird Orchid	52
Gumdiggers' Soap	23
Hebe elliptica	44, 45
Hebe salicifolia	45
Hebe speciosa	44, 45

Hibiscus diversifolius	7
Hibiscus trionum	7
Horned Orchid	57
Kaka Beak	19
Kunzea ericoides	14
Kunzea nichollsii	14
Kunzea scoparium	14, 15
Lady's Slipper Orchid	52
Large Flowered Clematis	4, 5
Large Flowered Spider Orchid	53
Large Leafed Coprosma	37
Leek Orchid	56
Lemon Wood	24, 25
Leucopogon fasciculatus	32
Lophomyrtus bullata	16
Lophomyrtus obcordata	17
Lophomyrtus pendunculata	17
Mangrove	47
Manuka	15
Melicope simplex	24, 25
Melicope ternata	24, 25
Metrosideros albiflora	8, 9
Metrosideros fulgens	8
Metrosideros robusta	8
Microtis oligantha	56
Microtis unifolia	56
Midget Greenhood Orchid	55
Mistletoe	11
Mountain Cabbage Tree	49
Mountain Flax	51
Mountain Holly	40, 41
Mountain Neinei	34, 35
Muttonbird Scrub	40, 41
Mutton Wood	42
Naked Phebalium	24
Native Myrtle	17
New Zealand Myrtle	16
New Zealand Passion Flower	6
New Zealand Privet	36
Oblong Spider Orchid	53
Odd Leafed Orchid	52
Olearia ilicifolia	40, 41
Olearia oporina	40, 41
Olearia rani	41
Orthoceras strictum	57
Paraxilla tetrapetula	11
Passiflora tetrandra	6
Phebalium nudum	24
Phormium cookianum	51
Phormium tenax	50
Pomaderris apetala	22, 23
Pomaderris ericifolia	22
Pomaderris kumerahou	23
Potato Orchid	57
Prasophyllum colensoi	56
Prasophyllum nudum	56
Prickly Mingimingi	33
Pseudopanax arboreus	27
Pterostylis banksii	55
Pterostylis plumosa	55
Pterostylis tristis	55
Red Mistletoe	11
Red Rata Vine	8
Ripogonum scandens	12
Rubus cissoides	10
Sand Coprosma	38, 39
Schefflera digitata	26
Seven Finger	26
Sharp Pointed Earina	57, Back Cover
Shining Coprosma	39
Simple Leafed Melicope	24, 25
Small Onion Orchid	56
Small Potato Orchid	57
Snowberry	30, 31
Solanum aviculare	46
Solanum laciniatum	46

FLOWERING CLIMBERS
(Pages 4 to 13)

LARGE-FLOWERED CLEMATIS
Puawananga
Clematis paniculata

Puawananga, child or flower of the stars, is the apt and beautiful Maori name of this clematis with its cascading showers of white flowers that remind the Maori of stars in the heavenly firmament. Their legends say that this flower sprang from the union of two stars, Rehua the father and Puanga the mother. Found throughout New Zealand, more commonly in lowland regions than upland, puawananga has the largest flowers of the nine-ten endemic species. It is a woody climber that often covers whole trees or shrubs. Sexes are on separate plants with pollination of the plants effected by insects, despite the flowers being both 'colourless' and scentless. The large size and prominent placing of the flowers on the vines is therefore important to attract such insects. Clematis on each leaf stalk have three broad leathery leaflets that are dark green at the adult stage of growth and some 10 cm long. The leaf stalks climb other trees by coiling their tendrils around the branches. Once firmly clasped to the host tree stiff internal woody tissue of great strength develops.

INDEX CONTINUED

Spider Wood	34, 35	*Thelymitra venosa*	54
Starry Hibiscus	7	Three Lobed Spider Orchid	53
Stinging Nettle	20		
Stink Wood	38, 39	Tree Daisy	41
Striped Sun Orchid	54	Tree Manuka	14
Sun Orchid	54	*Tupeia antarctica*	11
Supplejack	12	*Urtica ferox*	20
Thelymitra hatchii	54	White Rata Vine	9
Thelymitra longifolia	54	White Sun Orchid	54
Thelymitra pulchella	54	Wild Irishman	21

CLEMATIS Pikiarero
Clematis forsteri

Like the puawananga, this small white flowered clematis has male and female elements on separate plants, the flowers of the male being larger than the female. It is found principally in the North Island. To mark special occasions pikiarero flowers were once worn in the hair by young Maori girls as decoration, or by young chiefs who would place a flowering sprig in an ear. The leaflets which differ in shape markedly from those of puawananga grow only to 8 cm long and are very bitter to the taste. This circumstance was helpful to Maori women wishing to wean a child. They used to crush the leaves of pikiarero and rub the sap on their breasts, however they were indulgent parents as they often breast fed a child until it could run about.

NEW ZEALAND PASSION FLOWER Kohia
Passiflora tetrandra

While this is New Zealand's only passion flower, over six hundred related plants are to be found growing mainly in Central and South America. *Tetrandra* in the scientific name refers to the four-angled crucifix shape of the four male stamens. This high climbing vine may be observed as far south as Banks Peninsula, near Christchurch. The leaves of kohia are up to 6 cm long, dark green and glossy above, paler underneath. It flowers between November — January, the seeds are ripe about May. The flowers are greenish to cream in colour, succeeded by shiny orange berries the size of cherries with crimson to black seeds in a red pulp. These seeds were boiled by the Maori to express an oil used for medicinal and cosmetic purposes as was the oil or gum exuding from the stem of the plant. Wood of its vine stem was also cut green and left to dry and used thus as tinder to convey fire when on a long journey, little pieces burning like slow combustion matches.

STARRY HIBISCUS **Puarangi**
Hibiscus trionum

Another plant family but sparsely represented in New Zealand is that of the hibiscus which is most at home in tropical parts of the world. *Hibiscus trionum* is the smaller of the two. It graces some sheltered seaside spots in Northland and coastal islands at the top of the North Island. The other representative in Northland is the taller *Hibiscus diversifolius* (not illustrated). It is doubtful whether either are native to New Zealand, they are infrequently found due to stock browsing and human encroachment on their habitats. The leaves of puarangi are 5-10 mm long, spear shaped, coarse toothed and tapering at each end. The flower petals are pale yellow with dark purplish to brown centres. The seeds are black with hairy outer-covered capsules.

RED RATA VINE **Aka** *Metrosideros fulgens*

It is related that long ago an evil water demon, or taniwha, called Tunarua tried to seize Rau, the beautiful wife of the Maori folk hero, Maui. This great warrior sought out the taniwha to avenge the uncalled for insult and a terrific battle ensued which resulted in victory for Maui. He hacked Tunarua to pieces and cast the long tail into the forest where from its long and powerful sinews sprang, amongst other plants, the rata vines known to the Maori as aka. In scientific terms aka belongs to the *Metrosideros* species from the Greek words meaning 'iron wood' or 'heartwood', fulgens refers to the shiny leaves and albiflora (opposite page) to the white flowers of that plant. Neither of these rata vines strangles its support tree as does the lofty rata tree, *Metrosideros robusta,* of the New Zealand forest. *Metrosideros fulgens* grows in scattered areas throughout the North Island, in Nelson, Marlborough and the West Coast. It climbs up to 10 metres on host trees to reach the light and has shiny oblong leaves, inconspicuous yellow petals and orange-red flowers in clusters.

WHITE RATA VINE **Aka-tea**
Metrosideros albiflora

Distribution of the white rata is limited to Northland's kauri tree forests and southwards in scattered local lowland to lower mountain areas, as far as East Cape in the North Island. Its leaves resemble those of the red rata, being long, leathery and shiny, narrowed at both ends. The abundant white flowers cluster on the tips of the branches and the petals are small and white. Rata vines were much used by the Maori in everyday life. They lashed together the heavy frames and rafters of houses (whare) with them and the palisades of posts surrounding some villages (kainga). They plaited them into fish traps for catching the delectable eel, crayfish (lobster) etc. and the children made hoops (pirori) and swings (morere) with this versatile material.

BUSH LAWYER   **Tataramoa** *Rubus cissoides*

A New Zealand relative of the raspberry and blackberry the bush lawyer has similar fruit to the latter, but is not nearly so flavoursome. It differs also from the blackberry in having more elongated leaves with pointed tips, rather than rounded, though there are numerous hybrid variations. Like blackberry it is common over lowland country and acquired 'bush' lawyer as a nickname through its capacity to embroil the traveller, his horse and later the sheep of the settler in thickets of the plant growing in dense bush country in the nineteenth century. The barbs along its stalks and on the backs of its shiny leaves being so placed as to allow the tendrils to move easily up a support plant, but not so easily to be pulled down. Tataramoa, the Maori name, is also applied to gorse (furze) and blackberries and translates as 'bed of prickles' and — tongue in cheek — the alternate name, taramoa, as 'wait-a-bit', that is 'tarry-a-mo(ment)'. Both Maori and European bushman benefitted not only from its mildly flavoured berry fruit, but in regions where water was short from the sweet watery juice to be obtained in quantity from cut sections of its largest stems.

RED MISTLETOE **Pikirangi** *Paraxilla tetrapetula*

A small parasitic shrub with large bright red flowers, either solitary or 2–4 together that should not be confused with those of the rata. It has leathery green-yellow leaves and small yellow berries when mature. Favours forest country on both main islands and some off-shore islands.

MISTLETOE **Pirita** *Tupeia antarctica*

Pirita or puka grows to about the same height as red mistletoe, that is one metre tall. It is the country's most common endemic mistletoe growing on many different plants in forest country in both main islands. Its tiny flowers are green, tinged with yellow, and very fragrant. Its pale green leaves can have diverse forms and lengths on the same plant. Maori children ate the berries when they were more plentiful. The berries are white, often with pink tones, more rarely through to deep purple, sometimes all colours on the same branch.

SUPPLEJACK
Kareao
Ripogonum scandens

The tough, pliant, black or brown climbing vine stems of the kareao trail along the ground, encircling the trunks of trees, right to tops of them. They matt together in such a way as to make some lowland dense forest in New Zealand scarcely passable. It is hard to credit that this creeper is in the lily family. Green leaves with a metallic sheen sprout on a non-twining stem, the tiny flowers also being green with equally miniscule petals. The bright red berries are round with pointed ends and full of black seeds. Like the aka, the kareao is said by the Maori to have sprung from the tail of the taniwha Tunarua, while its tips hang down from fright experienced when Rata, a demi-god, confronted the fairy people who delayed him adzing a canoe. Kareao stems made ladders to climb cliffs, trees and enemy palisades, and very durable fishing pots and food baskets. A stretcher was made to carry the sick upon, while aerial roots of kiekie (opposite page) interlaced the frame.

GIEGIE **Kiekie** *Freycinetia baueriana (ssp. banksii)*

This climbing plant prefers swampy ground in the forest and coastal scrub besides streams and is found commonly in the North Island, less so in the South. It holds on to host trees by aerial roots, sometimes as thick as a man's wrist. In springtime high overhead in some friendly fork of a tree the male or female plants appear, for the sexes are on separate shrubs and are fertilised by birds transferring pollen with their feathers. The innumerable tiny flowers on the 7-15 cm long spiky inflorescences are enclosed by bracts or modified leaves. The innermost bracts, known as tawhara to the Maori, ripen in the summertime being then whitish in colour and resembling in taste a soft-flavoured apple with pear overtones. The ureure or patungatunga, fruit of the plant, ripen in early winter and the glutinous pulp, full of tiny black seeds, is divinely edible. So it was that the Maori had a supply of food from the kiekie both for summer and winter.

SHRUBS AND SMALL TREES
(Pages 14 to 51)

TREE MANUKA Kanuka, manuka
Kunzea ericoides

The *Kunzea* on these facing pages present themselves in such a diversity of forms from small shrubs to trees, thriving on the poorest soils throughout New Zealand, that comments can only be general. *Kunzea ericoides* grows to a large tree, up to 15 m. tall, is more common to lowland-montane shrubland, often alongside river banks. It has softer leaves, of less fragrance when crushed, than *Kunzea scoparium*. Its white flowers at 3-6 mm diameter are half the size of the other manuka and its woody seed capsules also smaller and narrower. A *Kunzea* variety known as *nichollsii* and named after a Captain Keatley, (not shown), has very small full-red flowers and small dark green leaves, and is popular in home gardens.

MANUKA

Manuka, kahikatoa
Kunzea scoparium

Kunzea scoparium can attain a height of 8 m. on lowlands or as readily be found as a prostrate carpet shrub on wind-swept sub-alpine hills. Its pointed, leathery grey-green leaves exude a pungent odour when crushed and earned the name 'tea plant' from the explorer Captain Cook who had them infused to make a beverage he described as a very bitter and agreeably flavoured tea, latter much used by whalers and white settlers alike. Cook also brewed up a beer from branches and leaves of manuka and rimu in the 1770's. A much rarer treat is pia manuka, or manna, a honey-tasting white gum exudation from the branches caused by the activities of a small grub. Manuka wood is red, very tough and fibrous. It was once used by the Maori for paddles, spears, adze handles etc. The simile 'Though small it is still a kahikatoa' or 'A small person should not be despised' sums up the character of its wood most aptly.

NEW ZEALAND MYRTLE **Ramarama**
Lophomyrtus bullata

Bullata refers to the blistered appearance of the leathery red-brown leaves. A shrub or small tree, up to 6 metres tall, growing in coastal and lowland forests in the North Island, also coastal Nelson and Marlborough. The leaves are glossy and round-ended, 1.5-3 cm long, with bubbly sections between the prominent veins making identification easy. There are four-petalled single white flowers of 1.5 cm diameter with many clustered stamens. The dark red fruit, 1 cm long and tasting somewhat like the acidic tropical guava, were once eaten by the Maori as an accompaniment to fernroot, that standard food item before the introduction of maize, potatoes etc.

NATIVE MYRTLE   **Rohutu**   *Lophomyrtus obcordata*

This myrtle can be 5-6 m. tall and occurs in coastal and lowland forest areas in patches throughout both main islands. The red coloured wood is tough and prettily marked. Rohutu branchlets are clothed in fine down, as are the undersides of the 6-12 mm long leaves which are thick, leathery, notched at the ends and dotted with oil glands. The numerous stamens, longer than the petals, make them appear that they are the main portion of the white flower. The round dark berries 6 mm long, like those of the ramarama, were collected by the Maori by shaking the trees after placing mats on the ground. *Lophomyrtus pendunculata* (not illustrated) is very similar to *Lophomyrtus obcordata* in distribution and description, but with flower stamens more like those of ramarama, un-notched roundish leaves and yellow-orange berries occasionally, as well as red.

CORK TREE Whau *Entelea arborescens*

One of a kind, unique to New Zealand, though related to the limes and lindens, the 'cork' tree gets its popular name from the nature of its light wood which is about half the weight of cork or balsa wood. The Maori used its wood for their fishing net floats and for a hand game. A small tree or shrub growing up to 6 m. tall in the milder coastal North Island districts north of Raglan and Tauranga, with pockets in Nelson and Marlborough. It has large, 10-20 cm long, soft, pale green leaves which, after the missionaries introduced handwriting, the Maori used as rough writing paper to send short messages, etching out notes with a sharp stick or nail. The white clusters of flowers, beautiful leaves, light to dark brown spiny seed capsules and gracious tree form have made it a popular garden species.

KAKA BEAK **Kowhai-ngutakaka** *Clianthus puniceus*

Nicknamed 'kaka beak' after the resemblance of the shape of the flower and seed pod to the beak of the native parrot kaka, this shrub was one of the first, if not the first New Zealand plant to be grown in Great Britain, being collected by Banks and Solander, botanists of Captain Cook's expedition of 1769. It is widely cultivated in New Zealand gardens too, as it was by the Maori. It is now rare in the wild, being confined to a few North Island localities from the Bay of Islands to Lake Waikaremoana. It reaches 2 m. tall, has silky haired branchlets, leaves up to 15 cm long, scarlet flowers 4-5 cm long and pods 5-8 cm long that are many-seeded.

STINGING NETTLE **Ongaonga** *Urtica ferox*

The Maori in one legend attribute to their ancestors Kupe and his companion Ngahue the introduction to New Zealand of their 'children' in the form of prickly plants such as ongaonga and matagouri, illustrated here. Certainly travellers who experienced the long stinging hairs of the one or the thorny spikes of the other may wish the parents had not produced such offspring. At least one tramper has died from the effects of ongaonga stings, just a light touch can lead to numbness for several days. The nettle can be a shrub or tree up to 3 m. tall, found on coastal to forest margin land throughout New Zealand. The glossy green leaves are 5-12 cm long, deeply toothed with stinging hairs — even the spikes of the minute green flowers carry hairs — as do the branchlets. The fruit is a tiny dry, brown nut.

WILD IRISHMAN

Though called by English settlers of the nineteenth century the 'wild Irishman', this shrub or small tree has latterly become better known by one of its Maori names, matagouri. Another Maori name is tumatakuru, roughly translating as 'standing-face-beater', a reminder not only of its prickly nature, but the use of its very hard mature thorns as needles to tattoo the face (and body) of the young Maori at puberty. Tattooing was considered a sign of mana and of beauty. The plant is abundant on the east coast of the South Island, less frequently found on the west coast of the North Island up to Waikato Province. Matagouri attains a height of 5 m., especially in hilly valleys. It is many branched with narrow leaves, glossy above and 10-20 mm long. The small sweet-scented white flowers have no petals. The fruit splits into 3 seed capsules when ripe.

Matagouri, tumatakuru
Discaria toumatou

COTTON WOOD **Tauhinu** *Pomaderris ericifolia*

A shrub growing mainly in the North Island to 1.5 m. tall. Bright green, curled back leaves and yellow flower clusters on branches shown here.

TAINUI *Pomaderris apetala*

GUMDIGGERS SOAP
Kumarahou *Pomaderris kumeraho*

The popular name arose from the practice of Northland's gum diggers of rubbing the flower heads together on wet hands to make a lather when soap was unavailable. Kumarahou grows extensively on the now-abandoned fields from which the kauri tree gum was dug. It prefers such poor clayey lowland soils, southwards to the Bay of Plenty. A shrub with rounded head, maximum height 3 m. The leaves are about 6 cm long, hairy, with prominent veins and midribs. They are dried and infused in Northland to provide an aromatic liquid useful for coughs, colds and general chest troubles. The many golden yellow flower clusters give way in time to thousands of capsules containing little green and silver seeds. The appearance of kumarahou in flower on kumara fields was one sign to the Maori that it was time to plant that sweet potato.

TAINUI (at left) *Pomaderris apetala*

Restricted in the wild to a few coastal areas from Kawhia harbour to the Mokau river which is a few kilometres west of Waitomo Caves in the North Island, tainui takes its name from the Tainui canoe, one of those canoes that brought the Maori to New Zealand from Hawaiki, their Pacific homeland, many hundreds of years ago. The trees that once grew at Kawhia are said to have sprung from the rollers or skids used for the canoe; those at Mokau from the green branches of tainui placed in the canoe as floor coverings at Kawhia when the canoe took some of the people to settle at Mokau. The Tainui canoe is also credited with introducing the sweet potato, the kumara. The shrub grows to 4 m. tall, is erect with many branches and has dark green leaves, wrinkled and sparsely clothed with silvery hairs above, light brown hairs below. The flowers are pale green and have no petals.

NAKED PHEBALIUM
Mairehau *Phebalium nudum*

'Naked' here refers to the absence of hairy down on this and other members of the Rue (citrus) family shown here. The leaves and other parts are very aromatic when crushed. Greenish oil from the mairehau shrub was combined by the Maori with various vegetable, fish and bird oils for cosmetic and medicinal purposes. Mairehau grows as far south as Thames in the North Island, to some 3 m. tall. Branchlets are reddish-brown, leaves willow-shaped, 2-4 cm long with red oily glands underneath. It has dainty white scented flowers in clusters; black seeds in small dry pods.

LEMONWOOD (Top right hand page) **Wharangi**
Melicope ternata

A shrub or small tree up to 6 m. tall with slender green branchlets. It grows in lowland North Island and Nelson/Marlborough forests. Leaflets are in threes, light shiny green in colour. Flowers are small and pale yellow, the seeds black and shiny. The Maori chewed the gum of this tree for bad breath and made a dart with the leaf, it was stuck into a reed stalk and held by the leaf, between thumb and fingers, then launched from a height, stalk first. The simple leafed melicope, *Melicope simplex,* differs from wharangi in having rounded leaves opposite one another. Widespread in both main islands, it attains 4 m. with slender branches. It has small green to white flowers and black shiny seeds.

LEMON WOOD
Wharangi
Melicope ternata

SIMPLE LEAFED MELICOPE
Poataniwha
Melicope simplex

SEVEN FINGER Pate *Schefflera digitata*

This small tree is found throughout New Zealand in the damper parts of lowland and lower mountain forests. It reaches up 8 m., having characteristically a light coloured bark and short branches. Sometimes it begins life as an epiphyte. The leaves are 7-10 fingered, up to 18 cm long. These were used by the Maori to call birds. A leaf was doubled up, placed between the lips, and the call mimicked of the particular bird sought by the catcher. The flowers are small and greenish, hanging in clusters. Juice of the fruit which are small and purplish black have been used to provide a purple dye as well as an ink. The wood of pate provided a base along which a stick was rubbed to make fire by friction before matches reached New Zealand.

SNOWBERRY **Papapa, koropuka** *Gaultheria antipoda*

The erect snowberry shrub can be about 2 m. tall, with thick bristle-covered branches and hard, shiny and saw-toothed leaves, 8-16 mm long. It thrives everywhere from lowland to montane elevations in open situations. Small bell-shaped white or red flowers in spring are followed by red or pink fruit. These were picked by the Maori when larger and more tasty berries were scarce to accompany the staple fernroot diet. A matter of being more attractive to the eye than pleasing to the palate.

BUDDLEIA COROKIA   Korokio-taranga
Corokia buddleioides

Restricted in locality and habitat to lowlands and forest margins from North Cape to East Cape in the North Island, this shrub attains about the same height as the golden corokia with which it readily hybridises. Its long (8.25 mm) narrow leaves are shiny, smooth and pale green above, silver white and downy below, assuming intermediate leaf forms in hybrids. Small yellow flowers appear at branch ends; the fruit are red to black. Korokio leaves were once used by the tohunga or expert in ceremonies to ensure that the food being steamed in the ground oven (hangi) was properly cooked.

GOLDEN COROKIA **Korokio** *Corokia cotonester*

Found growing on lowlands in the scrub throughout New Zealand is this rigid shrub with many interlaced and crooked branches. It has small thick, often round-ended leaves that are sparsely distributed on the twiglets. The 8.25 mm long leaves have fine white felt undersides. In spring korokio has a profuse display of tiny yellow star-shaped flowers with orange coloured centres that give rise to the 'golden' appellation. Another appropriate name given is the 'wire netting bush'. The fruit can be red, yellow or orange. The Maori fashioned wooden knives from the twiglets of this plant and used them to pierce the skin when it was necessary to treat battle wounds, accidental injuries etc.

FIVE FINGER   **Whauwhau**   *Pseudopanax arboreus*

Like seven finger, this tree grows to about 8 m. tall and is found throughout New Zealand. It also sometimes germinates as a shrub epiphyte on the trunk of a tree fern or some other small tree, sending its roots down to the ground. It prefers however coastal forests and open scrub country. The leaves usually have five 'fingers' and were employed medicinally by the Maori as well as woven into head bands as tokens of mourning at the death of a chief. The perfumed flower clusters bloom profusely in winter and the fruit clusters develop some months later, varying in shade from brown to almost black. Skids of whauwhau were once used when dragging heavy logs from the forest for house building or a canoe. The green bark was removed to reveal a slimy surface on which to slide the logs.

Three olearias of New Zealand. Muttonbird scrub, *Olearia oporina*, grows locally as a shrub or small tree to 6 m. tall along coastal Southland and Stewart Island. It is named for a sea bird, the titi, eaten by the Maori. The thick leaves are 7-15 cm long with white woolly undersides. The daisy-like flowers have violet centres. *Olearia ilicifolia*, the mountain holly, also has fragrant serrated leaves, attains 5 m. height and is widespread on both main islands. *Olearia rani*, the tree daisy, forms a shrub or small tree standing 7 m. tall. It is found in forests in the North Island and Nelson/Marlborough. The serrated leaves, 5-15 cm long, have white hairs underneath. White daisy flowers cover the plant in spring. Heketara leaves were used by the Maori to scent oil of titoki or kohia berries and were worn as headbands to mourn the dead.

TREE DAISY
Heketara
Olearia rani

MUTTON WOOD **Puheretaiko** *Brachyglottis rotundifolia*

Found only in South Westland and on Stewart and Solander Islands. A shrub or tree up to 6 m. tall whose 4-9 cm long leaves provide the muttonbirds with lining for their nests. These leaves are dark green, leathery and shiny above, covered with yellowish hairs beneath; the flower heads are yellow-tipped. At one time the puheretaiko plant got the nickname 'the Stewart Island postcard'. This goes back to the days when a visitor could write on the underside of a large leaf, place a stamp on it and post it off to a friend. Damp mail caused the Post Office to ban this practice. Maori children used to make leaf boats of the broad leaves and little drinking cups on Stewart Island.

DAISY SHRUB **Kohurangi** *Brachyglottis kirkii*

A shrub or small tree of North Island lowland to montane forests. It may start out life as a seedling on the ground or grow out of some cavity on a host tree as an epiphyte. The leaves are 4-10 cm long, narrow and light green with a tendency to fleshiness. The branches are quite brittle, the leaf stalks tinged with red. It has large daisy-like flower heads, 3-4 cm in diameter, with orange-yellow centres.

COASTAL KOROMIKO **Koromiko** *Hebe elliptica*

COASTAL KOROMIKO **Koromiko** *Hebe speciosa*

KOROMIKO
Koromiko
Hebe salicifolia

About 80 of the world's 100 species of hebes grow in New Zealand in a variety of places. Here are three of them, two coastal shrubs, *Hebe elliptica* growing to 2 m. tall on western coasts from Cape Egmont southwards in the North Island and eastern coasts from Otago southwards in the South Island. *Hebe speciosa*, the other coastal variety shown, also grows to 2 m. in height in isolated spots on the west coast of the North Island. The third shrub hebe is *Hebe salicifolia* growing to 5 m. tall and widespread on lowland and montane parts of the South Island except coastal Marlborough Sounds. The leaves of *Hebe elliptica* are 2-4 cm long, point-tipped and slightly curled at their edges which have minute white hairs. Flowers are white or bluish and lightly scented. The seed capsules are large and pointed. *Hebe speciosa* is probably the showiest hebe with its reddish-magenta flowers and 5-10 cm long, almost fleshy leaves. The 5-15 cm long leaves of *Hebe salicifolia* are thinner, much narrower and more pointed at the tips. Flower stalks sport fragrant white-lilac flowers, longer than the surrounding leaves.

The plant played an important role in Maori life. Sprigs of koromiko accompanied healing, planting and cleansing rituals when appealing to or placating departmental gods. The use of koromiko tips to cure diarrhoea and dysentary are well known to both Maori and pakeha, and to a lesser extent the use of the leaves as a poultice for various skin diseases.

BULLIBUL   **Poroporo**   *Solanum laciniatum*

This shrub or small tree, with poisonous berries when green, is a member of the nightshade family to which the potato also belongs. It grows everywhere in coastal and lowland habitats to a height of 3 m. intermingling with *Solanum aviculare* which it closely resembles. *Solanum laciniatum* has dark purple stems, rather than the green-purple stems of the other Solanum, larger and brighter blue-purple flowers with bigger centres and lemon-yellow berries instead of orange. Both species have variable dark green leaves 15-30 cm long. Maori and European settlers alike ate the berries when more plentiful, poroporo pies and jam were popular with both races. The leaves were used for rough clothing and for medications, they also garnished potatoes in the Maori ovens. The sap of the shrub was used to size canoes before colouring with red ochre.

MOUNTAIN SNOWBERRY **Koropuka**
Gaultheria depressa, var. novae-zelandiae

The low growing snowberry is found in mountain to alpine regions throughout the country, particularly on boggy ground. It has smaller leaves than the other snowberry species at 5-8 mm length, white bell-like flowers and white or red fruit. Early white prospectors and sheep musterers in the South Island sought out these berries from under the snow in times of need.

BUNDLE FLOWERED MINGIMINGI
Mingimingi *Leucopogon fasciculatus*

A shrub or tree up to 5 m. tall, openly branched, growing from North Cape to Canterbury, from the coast to mountain regions. Sharp-pointed, usually narrow but variable, leaves 12-24 mm long, green in colour but taking a yellowish tinge when full sunlight strikes them. *Cyathodes* (cup-shaped) refers to the tiny greeny-white perfumed flowers that hang down. *Fasciculatus* (arranged in bundles) refers to the flowers or branches that also hang in bunches. The translucent red berries are sweet to the taste and were formerly shaken onto mats by the Maori then placed in water so that the bad berries and leaves would float to the surface. The harvest was transferred to large baskets to eat fresh at leisure.

PRICKLY MINGIMINGI **Mingimingi**
Cyathodes junipera

This mingimingi grows throughout the country as a shrub or small tree reaching 5 m. high. The pungent sharp-pointed leaves, 6-16 mm long, of both the mingimingis were infused by the Maori and the liquid drunk for alimentary disorders. Numerous tiny greeny-white flowers arrive in springtime. The red, pink or white fruit of autumn times, attached singly to the twiglets, were also sought out and eaten by the Maori.

Three *Dracophyllums* are shown here on facing pages. The grass tree grows everywhere, sometimes to 12 m. tall, but just 1.5 m. tall at its sub-alpine limits. It has narrow stiff leaves, 10-25 cm long radiating out in grass-like tufts and 6-15 creamy-white flowers in clusters. *Dracophyllum latifolium* (right) was named spider wood by early settlers for the web-like pattern seen when the stem is cut. Identified by its candelabra branch shapes and plume-like leaf clusters. Found in the top half of the North Island. It has long erect panicles of reddish flowers that droop at the seed stage. The Maori made a type of flute from the spider wood by heating the young green stem over a fire so that the flaky bark could be removed by hitting with a stick and then hollowing out the stem. *Dracophyllum traversii*, the mountain neinei, may be confined to Nelson and the West Coast of the South Island. It is a stout-limbed tree attaining 10 m. in height.

GRASS TREE
Inanga
Dracophyllum longifolium

SPIDER WOOD
Neinei
Dracophyllum latifolium

MOUNTAIN NEINEI
Neinei

Dracophyllum traversii

A seed head of this plant is also illustrated.

NEW ZEALAND PRIVET **Hangehange**
Geniostoma rupestre

A bushy shrub that reaches 3 m. in height on coastal and lowland country in the North Island, Nelson and Marlborough. It has soft shiny green leaves, 4-9 cm long, arranged in pairs. The leaves are paler and duller green beneath. The greenish-white flowers have an unattractive odour that do not commend the plant to the home gardener. The black seeds emerge from small rounded capsules with pointed ends. When steaming fish or vegetables in the earth oven, the Maori wrapped hangehange leaves around this fare to give flavour to the food.

LARGE LEAFED COPROSMA **Manono**
Coprosma grandifolia

This shrub or small tree with slender trunk grows to 6 m. tall in forests of the North Island and northern South Island. The leaves are 15-20 cm long and 7-10 cm wide, thin and not very glossy. Grey-green flowers appear in clusters, orange-red berries likewise. A yellow dye made from the bark was used to dye flax fibre and whalebone weapons (patu) by the Maori. Manono leaves, like those of hangehange, were wrapped or plaited around food destined for the ovens.

STINK WOOD **Naupiro** *Coprosma foetissima*

SAND COPROSMA
Tarakupenga
Coprosma acerosa

Coprosmas as a species are chiefly to be found in New Zealand and grow in infinite variety. *Coprosma* (dung smell) *foetissima* (stinking) lives up to its name if one crushes the leaves etc. Fortunately other coprosmas are much less odorous. Naupiro is a shrub or tree up to 7 m. tall with leathery, 30-50 mm long leaves, white solitary flowers and orange berries. It grows throughout New Zealand. The Maori tohunga used naupiro leaves to fortell future events. *Coprosma acerosa,* or tarakupenga, is a flattened shrub of interlacing branches found to 2 m. high on coastal dunes everywhere. It has small, sharp-pointed *(acerosa),* very narrow leaves and solitary white flowers. The pale blue berries are the tastiest of the coprosmas to eat raw. *Coprosma lucida* , or karamu, has a height of 3-6 m and is common everywhere. The 12-17 cm long leaves are thick, glossy and bright green. Creamy white flowers and glowing reddish-orange berries are borne in large clusters.

SHINING COPROSMA **Karamu** *Coprosma lucida*

MUTTONBIRD SCRUB
Teteaweka *Olearia oporina*

MOUNTAIN HOLLY
Hakeke *Olearia ilicifolia*

MANGROVE **Manawa** *Avicennia resinfera*

Found only in tidal muddy creeks and estuaries from North Cape to Opotiki and Kawhia in the North Island the mangrove is a shrub or small tree reaching 8 m. tall. Its smooth leathery leaves are 5-10 cm long, olive green above and brown or grey beneath. The four-petalled flowers are small, ochre-coloured and slightly aromatic. The seeds of the yellowish fruit germinate before they drop from the plant. Stout, peg-like roots thrust up around the tree as 'breathing holes' to take oxygen from the air. Oysters mature on these roots, a fact known to the Maori who farmed these molluscs in past times.

MOUNTAIN CABBAGE TREE
Ti toi
Cordyline indivisa

The two pencil trunk cabbage trees and the third squatting dwarf variety are distinctive sights on the New Zealand landscape. *Cordyline australis,* at up to 20 m. tall, is abundant throughout the country near swamps, forest margins etc. from coast to mountain. *Cordyline indivisa,* at up to 8 m. tall prefers the mountains of both main islands and *Cordyline pumilio,* just 2 m. tall, is usually found under light scrub cover in the top half of the North Island only. Leaves of the common cabbage tree are 30 cm to 1 m. long and narrow at their bases, those of the mountain variety 1-2 m. long and more than twice as broad at 10-15 cm. The brownish green dwarf cabbage tree leaves are 50 cm to 1 m. long, but so narrow at 4-8 mm as to be easily mistaken for a grass or sedge. Flowers of all three are white in colour. Berries of all three are blue or bluish-white. Cabbage tree roots were eaten by the Maori, the leaves of the larger species made into baskets, garments, sandals, mats, twine for ladders etc.

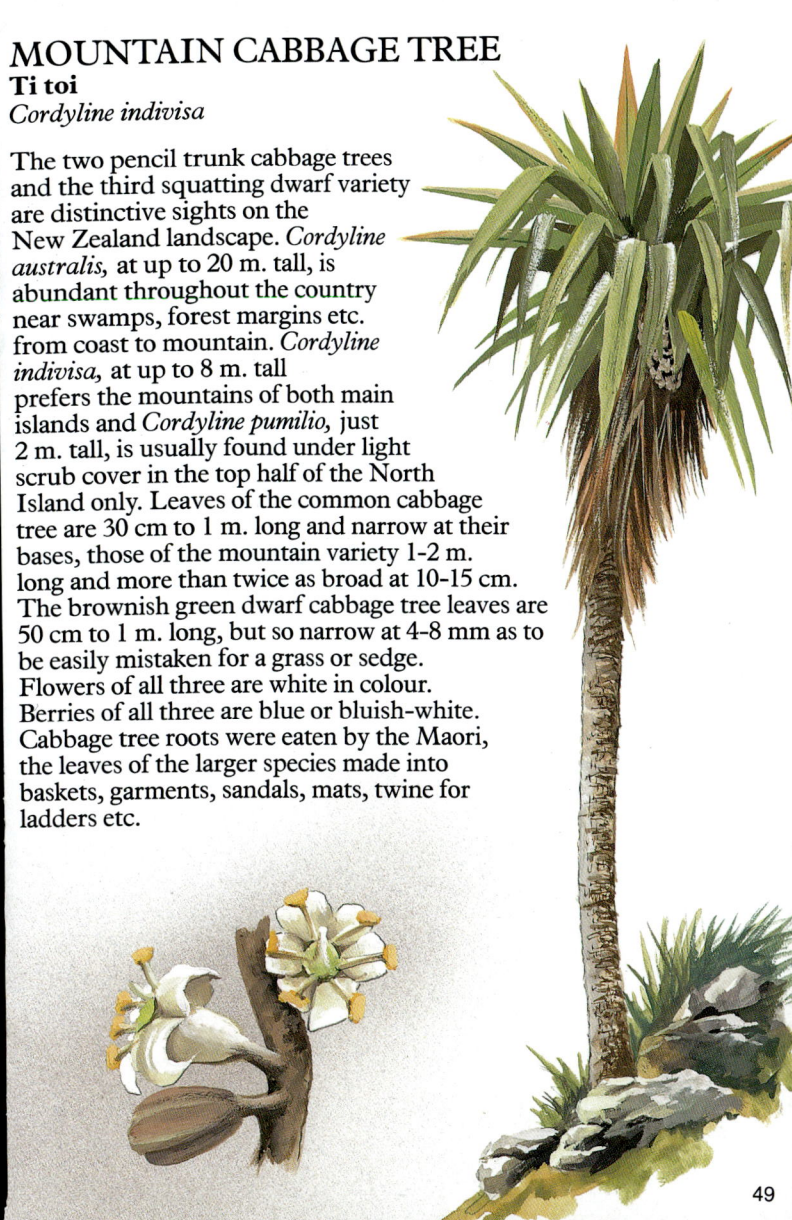

FLAX **Harakeke**
Phormium tenax

A common plant found growing in every habitat, particularly swampy ground throughout New Zealand. Its sword-shaped leaves measure 3 m. long at times, its dark flower stalks stand 4-5 m. tall with numerous reddish flowers, followed by erect 5-10 cm seed capsules which darken with age and open to reveal glossy black seeds. The Maori had names for some 60 varieties and cultivated them for specific purposes. It was the all-purpose plant. Leaves for garments required certain qualities and species. Baskets, mats, tops, hand poi, fish nets, sandals, bandages, rafts, drinking cups, toboggan, war shields, perfume sachets, all were made from the versatile leaves. Flower stalks were used as fire sticks, surgical splints, light fences and rafts. The roots in fish traps and medicines. Watery honey from the flowers supplied a drink and gum at the base of leaves was applied to skin sores and burns.

MOUNTAIN FLAX **Wharariki** *Phormium cookianum*

This flax grows from lowland to sub-alpine parts. It has less rigid and paler green leaves than common flax, about 2 m. in length. The dark flower stalks rise up to 2 m. tall holding yellowish-red or yellowish-green flowers, followed by drooping and twisted 10-17 cm long seed capsules containing glossy black seeds. Like harakeke, whararaki is used by the Maori to weave into garments but is not as valuable because the fibre is neither so long nor so tough. It was therefore most suitable for making mats to sleep on and shoulder straps to carry food on the back in bygone days. Many other usages parallel those of harakeke.

WILD ORCHIDS
(Pages 52 on)

LADY'S SLIPPER ORCHID (at left)
Winika
Dendrobium cunninghamii

Found throughout New Zealand. Epiphytic on trees in well-lit places.

ODD LEAFED ORCHID (at right)
Aporostylis bifolia

Found throughout New Zealand. Prefers damp forest areas.

GREEN BIRD ORCHID (at left)
Chiloglottis cornuta

Found throughout New Zealand. Likes shady damp places.

SPIDER ORCHIDS

OBLONG SPIDER ORCHID (at right)
Corybas oblongus

Found throughout New Zealand on sunlit banks to shady spots.

DANCING SPIDER ORCHID (at left)
Corybas rivularis

Found throughout New Zealand. Forest floor is its habitat.

LARGE FLOWERED SPIDER ORCHID
Corybas micranthus

Throughout N.Z. Forest floor, scrub and damp banks.

THREE LOBED SPIDER ORCHID (at left)
Corybas trilobus

Found throughout New Zealand. At home in scrub and on forest floor.

SUN ORCHIDS

SUN ORCHID (at left)
Thelymitra hatchii

Found throughout New Zealand in open and grassy places.

WHITE SUN ORCHID (at right)
Thelymitra longifolia

Found throughout New Zealand among rocks, on banks and open ground.

BLUE SUN ORCHID
Maikaka (at left)
Thelymitra pulchella

Found throughout New Zealand. Prefers clay banks, gumlands and boggy ground.

STRIPED SUN ORCHID (at right)
Thelymitra venosa

Found throughout New Zealand on boggy ground.

GREENHOOD ORCHIDS

MIDGET GREENHOOD ORCHID (at right)
Pterostylis tristis

Found on North Island volcanic plateau and locally down to South Island flat lands.

BEARDED GREENHOOD ORCHID (at left)
Pterostylis plumosa

Local to Wellington and Nelson. Found only on clayey hillsides.

COMMON GREENHOOD ORCHID (at right)
Tutukiwi
Pterostylis banksii

Found throughout New Zealand in forests and at forest edges.

LEEK AND ONION ORCHIDS

COMMON LEEK ORCHID
(at left)
Prasophyllum colensoi

Found throughout New Zealand up to alpine regions.

LEEK ORCHID (at right)
Prasophyllum nudum

Found from Auckland in the North Island to Nelson/Marlborough in the South Island on open lowlands.

COMMON ONION ORCHID
(at left)
Maikaka
Microtis unifolia

Found throughout New Zealand in open places up to sub-alpine areas.

SMALL ONION ORCHID (at right)
Microtis oligantha

Found in North Island high country and eastern South Island on both damp and dry places.